Praise for Barbara Cully's previous books

Under the Hours (JackLeg Press, 2012): "This is a new-century work, a voicing of Cully's tidal sense of the temporal, her premonitory stillness, written by desert- and sea-light, inscribing the endurance of loss, the necessity of vigilance. Her images are beautiful and precise, her sensibility profound."

—Carolyn Forché

That Place Where (Green Linden Press, 2017): "The semiotics of grief and landscape intermingle in Cully's powerful lyric elegy—so exquisitely particular, so brimming with heart."

—Karen Brennan

Also by Barbara Cully

A Place Where One (2017)

Under the Hours (2012)

That Place Where (2011)

Desire Reclining (2003)

Shoreline Series (1997)

The New Intimacy (1997)

Back Apart

Back Apart

Barbara Cully

For more information on this book or to order, visit www.jacklegpress.org

Published by JackLeg Press
© 2021 Barbara Cully
All rights reserved.
Printed in the United States of America.

ISBN-13: 978-0-578-87590-3

No part of this work may be reproduced or publicized in any form or by any means, electronic or mechanical, including photocopying, microfilm, recording, or by any information storage and retrieval system, without permission in writing from the publisher. However, authors maintain ownership rights of their individual poems, and as such retain all rights to publish and republish their work.

Library of Congress Cataloging-in-Publication Data

Cover design by Richard Every.

for my sister Jacqueline Cully

When desire is silenced and the will comes to rest, the world as essence becomes manifest. In this, the world is beautiful and removed from the struggle for existence. This is the world as such. However, contemplation and grace will not put the will to rest absolutely. It will awaken again. *—The I Ching*

And we go back apart across the field. *—Carolyn Forché*

Contents

Seaside and Seaside II / 1

Back apart across the fields / 5

To the lighthouse / 12

Myna Says / 14

What figures / 30

Meditation / 32

Between the buzz of a streetlamp and a cicada / 34

What happens to camp when the tyranny comes / 36

Like feathers trapped in amber / 38

There are five semiotic systems / 39

I remember / 40

Dead Troops Talk / 44

Eternally fixed afternoons / 48

Notes / 60

Note on the author / 61

Acknowledgements / 62

Seaside and Seaside II
for Patty

They were teenagers, not hippies, but they might have been: window-shopping the Pacific Beach head shops in t-shirts they'd slept in. Laughing, and almost waking the motel guests asleep down the stairs.

Some say it was the tambourine man—some, the hurdy-gurdy—but, in any case, the message was clear: there really was a summer of love. And there are some high water marks of the era still visible in the shoreline cliffs as they cave. Near Leucadia, and farther south at Ocean Beach.

My sister and I wandered near nightfall in the scratchy plaids of our uniforms, clicking a school ruler at a chain-link pace: meandering grounds we considered lush and a bit dangerous, well past six. Once some older kids asked if we were twins. One of us said yes; the other, no.

High school weekends we sunbathed for hours until somebody got mad at a blob of abalone tossed on a beach towel: Hey! Then a rounded piece of bottle glass, glinting and green. By sunset—not twins—we scoured the shoreline northward to the boulders: a series of leggy sprints in the spray.

Decades in—you're fast asleep but walking next to her again on a beach trail. Conversing in huddled whispers, ducking the shore breeze, lighting a tiny bonfire by the cliff. Look up: a dirt path. Look up: a train track. Look up: a scurry of figures shoving a gurney under a barricade of lights in the rain.

In the dream she takes off without warning, scaling a low hedge—and keeps going. I'm clawing hillside succulents, stones, and the gray roots of palms—trying to keep up. She power-walks through a sea of parked cars next to the coastal estuary—marching in flip flops through a dense eucalyptus canopy breaking finally onto a freeway pass overlooking a well-lit urban hive: a part of North County still called The Inland Empire.

Decades pass. You know, or think you know, a couple of European cities as a flaneur. You know, or think you know, a bit of history and philosophy, if not many facts. You understand a few geological processes and some of the cosmic elements: salt, boron, sand. And which can be used to fortify a seriously eroded cove—or to snuff a whole Chernobyl. These days, it's mostly in the language of wilderness discourse and human touch that you miss her. You think you know which 60s tunes can make a crooner of anyone. Or a birder. A whole American songbook.

II.

You now know how long it takes to cultivate giant succulents in the desert—and that the same cotton beach pants and woven hat will do. Blue agave as high as the house: giant prickly pear pruning themselves in the monsoons.

Late August, as you remember it, the wormwood carcass of the Mission Beach roller coaster—brainless and oily—loomed as enormous and out of place as a dinosaur.

Cotton candy. Vender shouts. Something greasy on a stick fried. A small girl vomits next to a ride called Cowboys of the Caribbean.

Our rented bikes propped against the beach wall where, laughing with some boys (a couple of loopy handstands), we're fine staying too long at the fair.

During the week of Santa Ana wind and that huge algae bloom, the riptide was as red as tomato soup. I learned quickly that when you get slammed against the bottom by a breaker, the brainstem flickers and none of the story quite congeals.

An earful of sand at cave depth retching then you dig deep into her shoulders frantic above the swells. *"We'll be okay,"* she holds on to you—nose to nose with you—going under. When you finally surface, voila! A buoy tossed into the spray by a couple of handsome angels.

Even though those patchouli-scented girls are getting hard to find, you're pretty chipper walking a stretch of rounded beach stones past a restaurant toward your car. Sandals clamped in one hand, a dog the size of a cat clamped in the other.

Back apart across the fields

for Beth Alvarado

I.

On the plantation, rumors about the director's motives (and later his family life) circulated among the raisin farmers and accountants, while everyone became increasingly concerned about the safety of the raisins themselves. In the evenings he comforted himself knowing there are preserved cadavers and brightly colored oxygen cylinders resting under ice on K12 and Everest. Even so, New Mexico is heating up second fastest behind Alaska. And, inexplicably, inflatable furniture is everywhere again. In the latest figures, endangered crocodiles on island nations have secretly started killing off humans. It's as if our whole culture has spilled its own bile in a hallway of cinema carpeting. Raw, rancid. Ripe for a second coming.

II.

Dark chocolate with a trace of blood

Could also be called Brazilian espresso with a trace of dried pepper: as the color I invented for the trim. Gray-on-gray lines drawn with house paint and late afternoon shadow. Mid-century modern, with duct tape fixing a dark trellis to a patio Dad would have dubbed "the lanai" in a real estate brochure. Coming of age in the 70s at a San Diego beach, there's not a lot of resistance when everyone on the boardwalk agrees it's probably the best of times. Later: much farther in, past bell bottoms and zories, a prose poem goes horror while a 2020 novel goes uncle tom's cabin among the croissant encrusted pages of the *Times*. There's nothing like the simultaneous loss of two dear friends. It gives us permission to grieve, to talk in darkness to David Byrne. The Tourette's of my new neighbor defines my apocalyptic sweetheart with her unfortunate theories about poison frogs and the convulsions of a chihuahua named Sabrina.

III.

Into the black forest

That was the day I tied my hair straight back in order to see my jaw against the skyline changing. Directly marching into what was left of the sun. In the lateness of the world, my solitary brain familiar and adrift. Eyes tight shut, nose enveloped by the lovely rot of pine. (I was trying to memorize the whole of a setting yet unclear.) We now know that in such woods pajama clad prisoners fled, already their own ghosts. Where in the line of fire pregnant women dropped toddlers briefly in the mud. Then the picking up and the moving on. Granddads-to-be as soldiers not yet twenty shoulder to shoulder offering tense or tender eye contact at the call to go back apart across the fields. Or to go over the top. To cross over to whatever was in store. Before enlightenment we trudge cliff edges hoping not to fall. After enlightenment we trudge the edges too.

IV.

Are you with me

Death knell in the desert on an ordinary sky-lit afternoon. That we wanted to unhear. That we wanted to suspend. A deep draft of catastrophic vapor from the event horizon of a peculiar midnight in March—or October. A January. All I never wanted to erase. All I never wanted to unhear; your voice unheard. Your molecules dispersing in a cave where every animal is both radiant and charred.

V.

Water never tires of becoming water; stones never tire of being stones

Ninety-five years ago, a South Dakota town was ripped apart by a subterranean mine fire, and the flames still burn under a boutique on Main Street called Centralia. We rely on the animal world, ancestors, land and sea, wind, carbon, lead, zinc, and a good bit of pharmacology to avert the recurring pain of such extraordinary danger. After a celebrated hog roast or a single lamb divided: my middle-aged grandmother lugging a wounded dachshund toward a retreating train. Such trials, encountered by all, but strategies for enduring vary from place to place. In central London, the grass roots effort to save the Horse Hospital from demolition failed after its basement gallery depicted altogether too much hair. When we calibrate, it's never certain how much time early astronomers spent calculating *astrological* predictions. But we do know something about Tavistock House, the onset of Ebola, 2001, and *The Blithedale Romance*. After Descartes and his dazzling explanations. After wheat fields. At the end of a long corridor. Torres Strait inhabitants are warned that the dioramas contain the names of deceased aboriginal islanders.

VI.

The leg and hoof of a horse

Just visible as if protruding through the stone. The fallen soldiers and their ligaments emerging triangular at the sharp edge of the relief. Just a fragment, really. That gray book in the shop you showed me on the street you showed me warned us not to begin by dreaming. You demonstrated daily it's fine to begin by walking. Okay to choose the village center or a thousand steps toward the cliffs of ash. She said the desert was her home. Yet over all the time before and since, home mostly when she wasn't there. She said be careful of the bus, the lift, the slicker streets on an Irish bright-lit day of wind. She was taking good care; rowing the boat really. In the sense that I was drifting. While bands of village people kept chanting louder nightly in robust unmelodic tongues. They followed us invisible from stoop to stoop. Wearing hoodies like ours, interrupting the rain. Approaching the next museum, a cobblestone chip entered me suddenly as a benign and gentle dream.

VII.
The echo of a word starts with a word

Between the rust of a street sign and a creeklet. Burnt-orange and crocus colored. The hard moon opened in a hedge of grass and gold. The temperature that seeks the fun in everything is *us* wrapped and walking. Sleet slowed down enough to feel. White-capped oceanic turbulence entwined with a white beard on a departed face. (I will miss you; come back; does it have to end?) Look: we almost made it. To handle the crowd, we walked directly against it. Last week or so. The Thames on our left. The Tate up ahead. In winter, in Wales, on the ferry, we hoped against hope. Without knowing what it means. We forgot how to swim. All foolishness is forgiven blowing a tin whistle into a tuft of song. The detail stuff is all there, for sure, in the guidebooks left behind on purpose on chairs. Ancestors upon ancestors in their tight gravesites. Leftover Eden scattered throughout the view. Barren Irish cliff-sides of zero trees and much rock. A tour bus driving us into and around fence lines of flagstone crushed. Whole rivers seeping down, and down, ten thousand years or more. After all of it, there will be another us. To face the planet like a hurricane. Like cheerful animals ravenous for more.

To the lighthouse

1.

But it's not what you think—I'm on the Pacific. And we're going to have to adjust for class, timeframe, cultural setting, wardrobe, generation, countenance, hair, latitude, and the like. And who would I be playing? At age 63, the matriarch, of course—my own moods and tragedies filled in. The same middle-aged persisting that blinks on like a porch light just as the laughter of the sandy children inevitably frays. (They grew up?) Yes, which means we're somewhere around page 197 in the middle section of the book (no need to check), and there is no lighthouse. Just myself made otherwise by all her pain, the considerable repetitions of an ordinary life that included embroidery. Wherein somehow oddly everything's askance. It's all just half a frame over and either right before or right after the current moment. Ready for a two-page extension of one's entire woodsy context. The subjective self's wavering pliés, poise, and tics. Its awe-fueled feeling tones.

2.

Soon my neighbor's son slices living flesh from a fish he's caught for bait, throwing the injured creature back to the waves. Lily, finally sailing for the lighthouse, inwardly completes the painting she's held in obsession from the start, now caring much more for shading than the paint. Even at the momentary end of one's life, it's better to go ahead and include the gradual autumn-tinged approach to the river— The river rocks, their mottled textures, the sharp and careful choosing of the river rocks—the altogether over-sized jacket pockets—until we detect and consider the smoothish, watery feel of both ecstasy and regret and cannot place it. (Is it late?) (It's late, right?) Until we detect a strong whiff of banal, fresh, and inexplicable English moss. Like the beginning of an Icelandic noir. Like the enormous thumbnail of a frightful Viking gripping iron and wood—just now turning blue.

Myna Says

It's possible to leave one's chairs and umbrellas exactly where they are, and the sky doesn't fall. The sky holds steady as we inch ourselves gradually out beyond the swells.

> Mynas are considered talking birds—for their ability to reproduce sounds including human speech while in captivity.

1.
Minutia and the passage of time

Twilight caught in a mesquite, doves cooing. The low voice of evening that includes Interstate 10, trucks roaring above the clatter. On Wednesday we were reading about John Ashbery's work, triple-jointed and colorful. Along with Weldon Kees' porch light coming on again. And staying on all through the night. Consider the woodpecker chiseling a sand dollar on the patio table. Consider the dove crafting an unfortunate nest in the rain gutter. Consider a canopy of treetops, opal twilight, bats lifting into a sky full of follies—a guy with a camera making a second or third try.

2.
The "yes" in yesterday as a series of extinctions

Neurologically speaking, if it's possible to re-live the moment before impact, it might be possible to re-live the impact itself. The human parietal lobe wants what the human parietal lobe wants. The hole *and* the doughnut; special access to dark-matter; a slice of the beforetime; tart pies served countertop with minimal conversation; a setting chosen for its muted amber light. We find that *heta* in the historical Greek alphabet is also the more recent letter *eta*. Its original duty: pronouncing the letter "H," a broad awning for talking about sound and the remembrance of sound.

3.

Open woodland fauna with strong territorial influences

A darting bevy of quail. Chicks the size of quarters. A gallop of pigeons—across a skylight. Captive mynas as stalwart members of the starlight family speaking to us in our own tongue—tongues. There are (were) ample colonies of glittering amphibians until minute fungi impaired the uptake of electrolytes, killing off all the offspring. When it comes to the newer extinctions, there are those that count and those who are counting. A handful of scientists bickering and sweating while adjusting pliable tubes. Tubes that bring water to the tiny waterfalls in the frog aquariums.

4.

An event counts as a mass extinction if it eliminates a significant portion of a planet's animal and plant life in a geologically insignificant amount of time

The golden frogs that thrive in captivity will never be given back to the wild, (a.) because a viable wild no longer exists for them amid forests of toxic fungi, (b.) because no one wants to do that, and (c.) humans exist for a geologically insignificant amount of time. At dusk the scientists go back apart across the fields—igloo tents aglow on the shrinking horizon. They reminisce their solitary childhoods amongst themselves. Hungry, they agree it's hard to remember earth has had five extinctions of the cataclysmic kind.

5.

Krakatoa. The afternoon of Sunday August 26, 1883

A numerical model for the Krakatoa volcanic eruption and the resulting tsunami produced an immense wall of water, higher than 100 meters. All of it propelled by a shocked ocean, basalt, and air. Dispersed worldwide, ash darkened the sky for countless ensuing years. Producing fuchsia and caramel twilights for many more. Geologic measurements show the island subsided (disappeared under water) into an empty magma pocket at the tail end of the cataclysm. Rather than being destroyed during the sequence of mass explosions. The initial crack was so powerful it ruptured the eardrums of sailors 40 miles distant. On ships in the Sunda Strait. Sea captains recorded human skeletons floating across the Indian Ocean on jagged slabs of pumice. Bobbing and drifting. Most eventually washing up on the east coast of Africa during the years after the explosion. To this day, a prominent geologist who works on a nearby island (some say he's just a hermit) doesn't work for the university or the museum. He lives on the grounds in a squat stucco cottage long since converted to office space.

6.

A well-crafted hunk of plastic effigy; a creature covered in hair or scales that once lived very large

When exactly humans first stumbled on fragments of the American mastodon is unclear. An isolated molar unearthed from a field in upstate New York and immediately sent to London. Still a nice place to explore. (London?) In North America at this juncture journeys were arduous and supplies short. Archeology scouts walked for days then set up camp on the east bank of the Ohio. Buffalo tracks wound the team down through the marsh from all directions. Hundreds or thousands of magnificent chunks jutting out of the mulch: to the eye of the observer who recently crossed the Atlantic, like the masts of ruined ships. Soon the gargantuan teeth became a trademark conundrum. (Resisting classification.) Not *elephas maximus*, not mammoth. Today the low-lying pasture where an intact *femoris* lay buried is a park in Kentucky called Big Bone Hips.

7.

Extinction as a beast no longer found lumbering along the rivers of North and South America

Laboriously reassembled; shipped to Madrid. Dr. Tassie opened a tall metal cabinet and placed the contents on his table. The remarkably preserved dents. Schlepped the length of the Ohio, yet barely understood. Even Thomas Jefferson ruminated: "Likely carnivorous; but if it's still out there somewhere, it won't be found in Virginia. This beast's hunkering in a remote alcove of the western continent as yet aboriginal—uncaptured and unexplored." When, around 1796, Monsieur Cuvier obtained sketches of a massive specimen from the banks of the Río Luján (west of Buenos Aires), he tagged it correctly as an outlandishly oversized sloth. Dozing at his table, the diminutive Cuvier was prone to mutter. He implored, "What has become of these enormous creatures for which there are no longer living traces?" (The question, in its formulation, answered itself.)

8.
Currently, the field of ethics and climate change concerns itself with scientific uncertainties, struggling to rank these as actionable objectives

In the town of Jumaytepeque, in Central America's dry corridor, crops and farmers are currently decimated by a plague known as *la roya* (rust) at higher and higher elevations. As the plateaus become warmer. As the semiarid Sahel region spreads ever wider across the African continent, a rag-tag group of teenagers make their way to Gambia crossing the Mediterranean from Libya. Each boy has a tinsel strength like the fierce glow of a flame under a bushel basket. The ubiquitous courage of sapiens DNA.

9.
At the event horizon of human ethics, we exist in a shadow of guilt

In the dream I'm talking to a couple of older teenagers in the parking lot of what's probably a university building (the Poetry Center?). It's after hours in deep summer with young kids milling about, looping around on skateboards and the like—purple sky—when one of the teenagers (lanky blonde, surfer hair) shoots off a number of rounds from a semi-automatic handgun, apparently for fun. He's having a good time, and so are his pals, while the smaller kids scatter abruptly in fright. Sparrows and doves shoot up fast through mesquites in a sudden clatter. I know the perpetrator, it seems, and approach him with what looks like a greeting, maybe even a partial hug, asking him how many rounds was that—about twenty? He says, "yep, about that," and I ask him to help me locate my car.

10.
Mice and men

The human brain has some growing up to do after it emerges from the pelvic arch and slips the rest of the way down. At around age two, the brain blooms in a way that means more cells and more activity than at any other time in a lifespan. All that blossoming makes for a bit of fun when toddlers express their ideas about nature and god. For instance, a child deciding that god's in the toaster finishing up the bread, or that it's a good idea to send up some bath bubbles to mommy who just flew off somewhere. An airplane is first enormous and then quite small. Contradictions and paradoxes result in curiosity and glee (not strife) until four-ish when the brain goes through an inevitable pruning process. The bustling organ elects to keep only neurotransmitters and pathways best for getting things done. At this point, human disunity makes its unfortunate entrance. All that loss doesn't happen without an audible crack of subdural lamentation.

11.

Just under the crust of consciousness, we understand cell loss as appropriately dire

Somehow (inexpertly), we develop a taste for the bitters and tannin of it all. We lose not just brain tissue but brain *capacity* while a fledgling consciousness prunes itself to merely. Merely what's practical to be conscious of (such as the self). It might be adaptive later on (age sixty?) to clip and shape the brain again. Imagine getting rid of overwrought ruminations as they surface at unpropitious times (upon waking). In this version, we carefully open a teak tool case, as if for an impromptu manicure. Then, with the rugged expertise of an Australopethicus Afarensis, we shave down the offending synaptic pathways like sharpening a flint tool. This might also be a good time to brush up on what happens when a tiny girl tosses her head back shrieking—as a butterfly twirls her around.

12.
In a steeply reclined position

First I was studying a branch framed by a slatted window, marveling at an emerald hummer as if in a trance. If sapiens were to vaporize tomorrow, it would be our teeth that would outlast—ossifying to tell the tale. In the meantime, a patient in a steeply reclined position faces the prospect of *losing one's teeth*. In Rome, inside the dank "chapel of bones" (the Capuchin Crypt), each wooden bin is a crib of femurs, scapulae, finger bones, wrists, skulls, and the like. The sign above the doorway reads: "As you are now, we were. As we are now, you will be."

13.

Tarantulas and the human unconscious

Some therapists call it the "known unknown"—or the familiar Keatsian veil of human trauma: the psychic tectonic plates of what Dr. Balint called the "basic fault" in his volume of that title. Something Rousseau would have dispatched quickly with an outbreak of morning paragraphs, walking stick raised. But, really, opening a spider icon on the desktop of human consciousness is enough to disrupt the start of any workday: welcoming Dr. Pandora into the break room with her cheese box of uninvited pests.

14.
Subterfuge and centrifuge as complimentary cosmic forces

Outsized dust balls the girth of comets, despite their youth. Post big-bang asteroids in advance of recorded history, and not entirely within the realm of speculation. Haute couture mathematics. What we get is the early planet bombarded for millennia with ice balls sufficient for three or four good-sized oceans. The salt water that will eventually express itself through the porous machinery of cell life until—past the autumn of the pharaohs but not of the patriarchs—we get a considerable distance ahead of ourselves. Artificial intelligence is not just a new language, it is yet another protein-fueled conversation. It exists at a familiar crossroads where the durable gates of Hades bar both entrance and exit.

15.

Mynas were medium-sized passerines with strong feet. Their preferred habitat was open country

Over time, in captivity, their voices became robust and direct—they eventually came to be considered gregarious. Then dangerous. Then endangered. If this last was due to their inculcation into spoken word, or because of the diaspora of poisonous fungi, remains controversial, some say by design. Still, the reports that mynas came to use tools (implements such as feathers and pens) are well founded, if classified. In any event, their counterparts in the coalmines were eradicated handily, which allowed for deniability whenever the question of fauna extinctions came up for an annual vote.

16.
Hunter S. Thompson was quoted as saying, "absolute truth is a rare and dangerous commodity"

What happened in the early years of the current millennium was something like a paradigm shift, but nothing that changed Beijing, Moscow, or Washington. What the intellectuals who would have gone to Spain with Orwell and Hemingway in the 1930s did with the species extinctions, water wars, epidemics, and nutrient-weak crops was in essence to gut the giant bear of modern culture, crawl inside, then etch the epic of a dying species on the bones of an even larger dying species. The famous centenarian, activist Greta Thunberg has said, "It was a different time. No one would do any of that today."

What figures

1.

That all mythic beings no matter how inelegantly drawn embody what is most desired and feared.

Just last week, several hand-wrapped beings, impeccably preserved, were exhumed from a Syrian tomb become bomb crater.

Among the miscellaneous rubble: some inexplicable black and white figures (circa 400 AD) and near pristine crayon drawings of… [to be determined].

Farther in, an open hand in silhouette—a human cameo as yet undated and heavily scrawled over by vandals in the years predating the current conflict.

The smallest of these figures, probably female—or a child—was found quite intentionally bent over at the waist, possibly in prayer.

A fallen figure is canted toward the cave entrance, its bird-like mouth agape as if calling out in lament or provocation.

2.

But how can we assign intention to the maker (let alone the figure)—so long since?

(Because we are kindred.)

Baffling: records conclude infanticide is as common now as then.

The documentary impulse is as fervent today as ever: the desire to look and to look away.

3.

These things as such (in situ) proving that 'time immemorial' is not unmarked, nor undone, by its own continuum.

It figures that what we are, lava-like, pours over strata, errata, and data.

While what we desire most is the repeated gesture (carnal, thirsty, beckoning), grounded in a recurrent feed.

Meditation

for Jen and Emmy Casale

I.

It started when I wanted someone to grab me and say.
It started when the woman across the street finally got her
 children onto the bus.
It started with a couple of teenagers in a car tweaking.

It started with a photo that might have been Patti Smith but was actually Uncle Lavern on a quick trip to Tijuana with us kids.

It started with confusion about who all was going and who was staying back. On the beach, it started with something washed up but not yet dry.

II.

It started down the hall under a blue archway,
with an infant propped next to a three-year-old.
It started after calculating one decimal out to an extreme.
It started including all the cars you ever owned.
It started becoming a cameo—like a vignette—edited down to a parable about love.

III.

It started at a breakfast of almonds, caraway toast, and figs—with a crock of enthusiasms, and yens, becoming a desire to rake and sleep.

IV.

It started with winter doing what it wanted with the roses. With a moment of leisure between sisters on the patio: leaning into one another with starry attention borne out of playing. It started with a sea squall battering a boat of innocents out to a vanishing point. Two humans and one squid entwined in a growing swell. The entire Pacific a convex whole.

V.

It started with the southwest fading into mourning—with us unpacking a vehicle of dogs and kids coming to rest in a courtyard of palms and fronds. It started with the joy of ordering breakfast off a menu decided hastily before bed.

Between the buzz of a street lamp and a cicada

Red-orange and crocus colored.

The open moon in a clot of gold.

When the world began.

The temperature that seeks the flaw in everything is this desert

slowing down enough to feel.

Passion entwined with an idea of face, faces.

I will miss you, come back, does it have to end?

Look, we almost made it.

To follow the crowd, we walked against it.

I hope we didn't forget how to swim.

The important stuff is all there—for sure—

a stone garden scattered throughout the view.

A fire stick passed down to us ten thousand years ago in a

hurricane.

A squat of hungry drummers pummeling for more.

What happens to camp when the tyranny comes

If camp is the index to how much tyranny there is in a given culture at given time, we've had a large dose of it (tyranny) for quite some time. Our careful attention to trade winds, cruelty, and messaging was almost a game, or might have seemed like a game. Until it went algorithmic like a riot on the capital. But in all the important regards—general health, general understanding—we missed it. Tyranny came in on cat feet in a season during which we felt inured to tyranny. (Kind of cozy.) There was nothing melodic about it. (So what do we do?)

We bundle our remaining belongings and children and go back apart across the fields. Never a good plan to trudge with a scarecrow's gait; never a good idea to haul a makeshift canoe back to a smoldering city. We're not bodhisattvas in burlap muumuus— not sudden laurels or pillars of salt. And, in these times, not the expectant meek—even if the notecard you prepared in advance reads, "The light, it already fades, Mr. Bones."

Kristallnacht does not sound lyrical even as repeating. In the photograph, ice and glass crashed to the streets—and eyeglasses crashed to the streets from the heads of onlookers—like silver scales. In this chapter, "going back apart across the fields" means you have a dead girl's chance in hell.

A bit farther in, you're tugging distractedly at a silk bra strap (your own), slinking off a dimming stage deafened by a raucous cowboy ovation. Somewhere inside you're thinking, "It's not too late to skirt the dragon-stained erotics of anger." You remember your first crush…his porchful of wisteria wafting. You remember his scent, a familiar heat ripe with DNA, confirming how thirsty for love you really are.

Like feathers trapped in amber,

it's getting hard to get out. Commuting to and from today by taking a long drive—wondering if Integrated Wound Management on East Speedway would be worth a try. Pondering the Greek origins of Red Wing Shoes. Feeling ultimately uncritical about a coffee dive called The Human Bean while one's chest becomes a rather shallow place, impossible to ford by walking or riding an animal or vehicle. Longing finally to be a brook. A freshwater stream smaller than a river. A recurrent impulse to fill up every empty space before moving on.

Come to think of it, some of those opaque lines were true: "return to a place lit by a glass of milk." That line in Hemmingway about "letting a little air in." You understand why you cannot understand a house in neighboring Syria that suddenly explodes. You suspect that most language hides incendiary devices that reinforce hierarchies and defy decorum; that eating utensils will soon be apocryphal; that the matted carcass the cat brings in might be a new way of communing with nature and doing your part.

There are five semiotic systems—

the linguistic, the visual, audio, gestural, and spatial. They consist of letters, words, drawings, photos, videos, sounds, music, facial gestures, and the design of space. We know that all language is a structured system of arbitrary signs.

Symbols, on the other hand, aren't arbitrary. Ambiguous as they might seem, a symbol is never completely arbitrary (irrational). A symbol maintains a common sense relationship with what is signified. And there's an overt distinction between language and speaking.

Speaking is an activity of individuals, and language is the social manifestation of speech—evolved from the active display of speech. Bob and Judy speak a language created by a multitude of speakers who came before them who are now for the most part departed.

Bob and Judy are ignorant of most of all that and insert themselves into everything they say. If we play the game Jenga with Bob and Judy, we can attempt to extract all the offending blocks so the purity of the structure remains. In essence, we'd like to pull the offending cruelty out from under everything they say.

I remember

for Beth and Fernando Alvarado

I remember everything I see, so for a long time I didn't understand cameras. But after sixty I do.

Forty years is a long time for not enough time with someone and pretty soon someone might say *rather briefly*. Whatever that is supposed to mean.

Something unspoken is what we both know about the roaring light. Absolutely repeatable.

Walking, we can imagine each other easily. Such ease that even that rattlesnake over there, dying for an interpretation, does not intrude.

Exhaling should come with a set of instructions translated from an ancient text. (Oh, it does?)

Long periods of nothing then the world come back to me in a dog's voice.

Like the yellow of the absent sun come up the stairs as a blonde
 mutt seaside.

Looking for clear skies tonight getting down to the freezing areas.

Breaking news that the Chinese are heavily video surveilled, and some don't care. Jimmy cracked corn, and most did not.

(Just saying.)

Finding oneself having to pause, take breaks, stop reading for a while and pull oneself together. (But did reading it *help* you?)

(The raven's response was not far in coming, that gray book told me—that sparrow chick told me.)

I was imitating someone there—then he told me he was imitating someone there too—a cartoon—Olive Oil or some such—but that could have been just reaching. More like Olivia de Havilland, really.

We want to remember none of this is theatrics. Most of it is information, which is an asset to someone doing something they wouldn't otherwise be able to do. Still, when you get something right—cleanly right—it enhances everything.

Your face superimposed over your face in the brilliant light. On the beach the self as a patch of skin against a background rising.

A faint voice welcoming us back to fresh air where we never ever want to fight a war like that again.

A case for growing old, older—gracefully as someone's father looking for stones and the evidence of stones.

A case for making the care of found babies delicate and easy instead of mired in the heartache subterfuge will require.

Stupefying. The way the culture of the army works up a narrative about "Iraq in general."

Like the one about a more just, verdant, and peaceful world.

There now. There now-now.

You, carried off, quite a bit, even fully, as if by a strong wind. You tumble and tumble. Your face cracks a smile as *it* cracks in the autumnal fires you become as you breathe. There now. There now-now.

Upon waking, you will remember everything and feel light upon waking, in the morning.

Truth be *told and told*, until there erupts just as much emphasis on the telling as there was on those irksome meanings.

The water lilies of summer are gone, but the water lilies of summer are never *ever* gone nor are they *anywhere* but in summer, Sillies. The evidence is clear.

At the end of the garden rocks a hammock. *Damn it.*

In particular, he gave and gave, understanding the birds as absolutely as his dreams and the stars, meaning *our shared stars*.

He jumped out of the plane just once, always conscious of his treasures. He knew that place well. As if visiting it often.

Dead Troops Talk

> God said to Abraham, "Kill me a son"…
> Abe says, "Where do you want this killin' done?"
> God says, "Out on Highway 61."
>
> —Bob Dylan

(Bat tucked,

in a delicate bridge arch much larger than this room,)

for long periods

what awaits is far off.

Hovering, in company,

      in this haze of being skin

      detonation row

      versus bent alley alcove or ravine

Not here, or here.

The shadows evaluating

The brief mourning it takes to destroy a human being

By mid-afternoon

Impossible

To go back apart across the fields.

Or the gathering of firewood

The casual running of a knife blade under a fingernail

These woods this river its meadow

Not possible to do something about summer

(Evening coming on again)

Or something about dinner.

In this coarse about-face turn around of air

    severe as any afternoon

        with its harsh desert shadows.

This one's belly's open to conversation

Putting up a fuss,

Putting on an air

as one gruff beast

Shoulder shucked to quick, to stub.

Cranium opened

He propped in the road now with something brief (and funny) to

say about what the traffic will bear

      (at whom directed)

Pliéd and imploded right here

As one put wet into a shallow bucket or spring

Caps and hair aloft

The brief backward hiss of intestine until fully drowned.

Disc-broke,

mountainous chest not so much puffed as tummy melt

      cartwheel plopped and all too reeled.

      At its greatest incline gravel angles quickly downward past

repose and settles

the reaper's contracts fresh with dying.

Well-lit shouting amongst the near departed

Jokes for starters

A skeleton walks into a bar slams down a dollar and

rock crushes scissors cuts paper covers rock

It only hurts when ma

no hands look don't touch me now.

"Eternally fixed afternoons"
—Frank O'Hara

I.

On the third Wednesday in ordinary time

half a woman, really, off a balcony

      in the early December of another hemisphere.

Danced or frozen

amid a well-placed healthy skepticism:

the letter "P,"

where birds listen intently (how dry it is).

Where among spines, hair, lead, sand

and shellac—a garden gate stands amid a plain

triganomally. That place where

we—banished to be certain—but

bound to be people

again soon.

II.

If and very

Ocean green and sky white. Those starlings get as flurried as we do (?). The "jump from" as little effort as the "slipping off." In sleep, the peeled back as much progress as tipped, forged or bent. Not now, but when and later, if and very, she said (inadvertently swerving for a moment from the day's topic).

Shore-long voices: if-we-had-not-been, if-we-had-not-been, covering a small bit of the pulsing, hemispheric skull of world, crossboning and plate-breaking, forcibly making the voice of god an audible chiaroscuro against cloud walls, or?

Weed rock and the crumbling cliffs. Bent spine, or pine. Umbrella sky.

III.

Eluvial

This, an expanse of beige sand before the red stepping stones placed in a curve, showing a bit of direction, a stepping off and then an arcing toward. During the time you were used to going over, crossing over, there was sometimes water in the wash, sometimes not, and, if we press it, a cow or two scattered in the green (expanse of field). At that time your secret was full. At that time you borrowed fullness from it. And from the way your face both filled and emptied too, cut as it was by harsh desert shadows. This, before you hauled in the stepping stones, thinking they could in almost reaching suggest (like a comma) a way of walking towards. There is, or is no longer, a configuration of boulders gray and green across the canyon. Years, and the eye papery; an arid breeze allowing arrested figures to spread their colors and dissolve.

IV.

Confessing to a long-held disbelief in the laws of physics

(A general problem with the Horse Head Nebula or something
    more specific?)
A deep suspicion of one thing's following another.

Someone sends you a glassy photo of a suspended wave amid some endless flapping. A palm near the English end of an articulated drive.

One thing then another, then a spectacle rising as a cascade of
    boulders gray and green.
(A lava-infused tsunami at its pointy height just tipping.)

Hands mushroom beige and under-hydrated.
As weak and fragile as your bicycle's cracked and brittle parts.

Somewhere up ahead a daft teenager's going, "by gawd, if it isn't
    a skull."

(The twinkling sounds of summer.)

A robust bracelet of Venetian glass burst into fragments on your arm.

V.

Three views of a sunset in March

Not only your dreams but occasionally the dreams of others will punctuate the ending day. Amid the closing day and its violets, you want to look around for a teacher or helper. As the massive ocean first casts then absorbs the sun's fading rays, you bounce a bit in your corridor, these thoughts and no others, a sense that what is lacking in your condition is what is required to go on, while you go on. Turning under the lengthening shadow of a palm (on your heel) to resume a party you've had minimal part in up to now…and come to walls of books next to the under-used bathroom, all of them alphabetized. As the day closes, as it goes, some years from now, someone else finds your name and turns its opening page.

This while you live, not an apology for how you will die. One brick and then two. No magic in allowing the rain to accumulate faster than the excuses. If we proceed, there is caution, if we hold back, pity. It is not necessary to claim the emotions bestowed on, or attributed to, you or near you. Like a traffic, the words used to name these conditions will clot then disperse, clot then be remembered, clot then experience a failure or inability to clot anymore.

When you are in the colors (lost), you will hear their sounds. When you are outside the colors (found) you will not. There is a blankness of, an absence of, sounds when you are outside the colors as the colors erupt brilliant before they fade.

VI.

Because you don't know that mourning branches,

because you do—and that peculiar branch of periwinkle
    that winkles and no doubt appears in colors upon colors.

Those of us are leaning into a place where—
    into the general direction of
    an idée / deus,
de / day.

You know the drill.
    Anyone who wheresofar and beseechyond such that
    joy is the final revenge-ugh.

Sí and oui as reflexive as those sweetly
forever muscles worn of yourn.

    Moi equals
    to ask and ask.

VII.

First he was subdued and then he was rise, and when he was begotten, and aft, he was still rise.

Now gunned-to-air, as plumed as wood, wooed and placed with care like a bell's tongue (laid on its side) and tipped toward the earth at once. His body no more careened or caterwauled. No more runaway truck or carved-up voodoo effigy or vase. No longer hurricane-whipped or creaking gate. Not a pent-up storm or baron full of whiskey. Wailing in the street. He who arced and strained and rode and swam and swam anon. He that travelled on. His days all mined, once rich, now coaled, and cold. All bye and bye.

But what a sweet creature always inside him bloomed. Even when all was gasp and lunge. So brave to greet his allotted work and phlegm. All that incline and purge each morn. Blood-full his lungs as all those mere hours now be longing. A mouth of sighs hung on to life then whither-whisked to whisper tunnel end. Knuckle deep, my face is so *saw* and *road*. I cast it down. This angled brow of mine is plucked to done. Forgive me— All brunt, I interrupt the music to ashk and ashk.

Notes

"Seaside and Seaside II" is for my big sister Patty.

Sections of "Myna Says" owe a debt to Elizabeth Kolbert's *The Sixth Extinction* for information and passages borrowed, altered, adapted.

"Between the buzz of a streetlamp and a cicada" is a composite poem that includes lines from my students in Honors 222.

"Dead Troops Talk" is inspired by Jeff Wall's "*Dead Troops Talk (A vision after an ambush of a Red Army patrol, near Moqor, Afghanistan, winter 1986.)*" Transparency in lightbox. 1992. Two lines echo Louise Glück and John Ashbery.

"Eternally fixed afternoons": part one is inspired by the mixed-media work "Garden Gate" by Kyle Johnson. Parts six and seven are in memory of Morgan Lucas Schuldt.

Note on the author

Barbara Cully is the author of two poetry collections from Penguin Books: *Desire Reclining* and *The New Intimacy*, which won the National Poetry Series Award; and two collections from Kore Press: *Shoreline Series* and *That Place Where*. In addition, she has published *Under the Hours* (Jackleg Press) and *A Place Where One* (Green Linden Press). She is co-editor of two writing textbooks *Writing as Revision* and *Entry Points* (Pearson). She taught for many years in the Department of English and Honors College at the University of Arizona, has been a guest writer at the Prague Summer Writing Program, and was recently awarded the title Distinguished Adjunct Professor by Golden Gate University, San Francisco. She was born in and grew up in San Diego, California.

Acknowledgments

Many thanks to my dear friends and readers: Beth Alvarado, Victoria Garza, Boyer Rickel, Ginny Threefoot, and Kim Westerman. I'm grateful to Jennifer Harris, editor and visionary.

I gratefully acknowledge the editors and staffs of the following publications in which some of these poems first appeared (some in previous versions):

Under a Warm Green Linden, 2020: "Back Apart across the Fields" (two sections).

Meluzína (Prague Program online publication), 2018: "Myna Says."

Green Linden Chapbook Series, *A Place Where One*, 2017: "I Remember."

Green Linden Chapbook Series, *A Place Where One*, 2017: "Eternally Fixed Afternoons" (parts I, V, VI, and VII).

Zocalo Public Square, 2013: "On the First Wednesday in Ordinary Time."

Cutthroat, 2010: "Dead Troops Talk."

Eleven-Eleven, 2010: "If and Very."

Bayou, 2009: "Three Views of a Sunset in March."

Other Titles

jacklegpress.org

Under the Hours. Barbara Cully

Hallucinogenesis. D.C. Gonzales-Prieto

Trapline. Caroline Goodwin

This is How I Dream It. Jennifer Harris

Men in Correspondence. Meagan Lehr

Observations of an Orchestrated Catastrophe. Jenny Magnus

when i am yes. cin salach

Two Thieves and a Liar. Neil de la Flor, Maureen Seaton, and Kristine Snodgrass

Genetics. Maureen Seaton

Undersea. Maureen Seaton

The War on Pants. Kristine Snodgrass

www.ingramcontent.com/pod-product-compliance
Lightning Source LLC
Chambersburg PA
CBHW022021290426
44109CB00015B/1263